3 Day Guide to Dublin

A 72-hour definitive guide on what to see, eat and enjoy in Dublin, Ireland

3 DAY CITY GUIDES

ISBN: 1507828381
ISBN-13: 978-1507828380

"Life is either a daring adventure or nothing at all."
    – Helen Keller

CONTENTS

1 INTRODUCTION

Phoenix Park. Photo by Roberto Taddeo

The beauty of Dublin is far from superficial; reaching far beyond what the eyes can see. It would be difficult to describe this city in one word as Dublin conjures up a myriad of images, interwoven with rich history and culture, but one word fits perfectly to define this gem of the "Emerald Isles", it is *extraordinary*! Dublin is a destination that is throbbing with passion, brimming with life, and overflows with energy. It pulsates with daily action and bursts with creativity.

Discover for yourself the wonders of this city with an exceptional past. Dublin, Ireland's capital, is located on the East Coast, stretching along the Irish Sea in a half moon shape. It lies at the mouth of the River Liffey in a land area of approximately 115 square kilometers. Dublin is bordered to the South by the dramatic Wicklow Mountains and is surrounded by flat farmlands to the north and west. The Liffey River cuts the city into two, namely the Northside and the Southside. This division does not only exist geographically, but culturally as well during the earlier times, when the working class occupied the Northside while the Southside was populated by the middle to upper-middle class strata of society. Over the years, this social division disappeared and has become indistinguishable.

Bask in Dublin's rich culture and tradition in a city that has a long-standing passion for creativity. This is showcased through their arts, music and undoubtedly, through their close affinity to prose and poetry. Remarkable writers were all born and raised in Dublin, including James Joyce, an Irish novelist and poet who is considered one of the most influential writers in the modernist avant-garde era of the early 20th century; Oscar Wilde, a writer and poet who became one of London's most popular playwrights and Bram Stoker, the famous author of the Gothic novel, Dracula. There's countless renowned Dublin writers, composers, novelists, dramatists, actors and actresses as well as musicians spanning centuries of sharing their talents and crafts with the world. The world-famous band U2 also hailed from Dublin.

Mapping out a trip to explore Dublin can be far from the usual. Unlike other European cities, this is one place where you cannot travel along the "dotted lines", encouraging you to go beyond the norm. Dublin offers a thousand and one discoveries with a complete mixture of the old and the new. Its a place where traces of diverse cultures can be found all over the city, deeply ingrained within the inner recesses of its edifices and alleys.

Smoking break. Photo by <u>*Giuseppe Milo*</u>

Since most of the structures of the bygone eras have either been refurbished or restored, the originals can no longer be seen. You may need to look further, where exploration may lead to you to priceless discoveries. It will be an adventure to go and find hidden rooms that still remain intact inside Dublin's modern buildings. You may even be surprised to know that some pubs and restaurants are the remaining parts of churches and monasteries, refurbished and converted into fine dining halls.

But, there are still several cultural mementos and historical artifacts scattered throughout the city. An original stone wall built during the Medieval years can still be found along Lamb Alley, right in the heart of the city. This part of the wall that surrounded the city during the 11th century, used to have gates to allow passage to and from the castle. One of the original gates still exists along Cook's Street. In Christ Church Cathedral, which is one of the most famous buildings in modern Dublin, many relics and artifacts, as well as beautiful objects that the church owned, can be seen. Dublin Castle will give you a glimpse of its medieval past through the only remaining fully intact tower in its midst. This castle was once erected beside the "black pool" which disappeared after the River Poddle was diverted from the castle. It used to be where the castle garden now rests.

At the corner of Mary and Abbey Street, a monastery once existed. Today, you will no longer see the original majestic structure as it was brought down during the 15th century. Its stones and materials were used to build other structures in the city. However inside one of the edifices in its exact location is one of the original chambers of the monastery, the Chapter House, reputed to be one of

Dublin's best kept secrets.

Despite all its changes, the city still holds many clues to its historic past. The road to discovery will further be unveiled as you view the landmarks of the then and now, allowing Dublin to tell the stories hidden in its nook and crannies. Don't be surprised to find yourself simply sitting in one of the parks and imagining how Dublin looked a thousand years ago.

Today, as a young city, with 40% of its population below the age of 30, this is a place with a young, tenacious populace that has an infectious vibe of positivity and fun. The mood is vibrant and exciting with an ever-growing economic resurgence as the biggest global names and players in the information technology fields including Google, Facebook, Twitter, LinkedIn, AOL, eBay, Microsoft, Amazon and Yahoo, have set up their headquarters here.

History

To understand Dublin, it helps to know the city's origins and how it came into existence. Early Dublin is a far cry from what you see now however traces of the past can still be seen in some parts of the city, echoing of days gone by. Dublin was initially inhabited by the Vikings in 841, a boat-riding people who originated from Denmark and Norway. The earliest settlement called Dyflin or Duiblinn in Irish was erected, which means "black pool" referring to a black tidal pool where the River

Poddle entered the Liffey River. Viking houses were very simple, made of wooden materials, with no chimneys nor windows, perhaps to maintain the temperature inside. Many of the Vikings were craftsmen like blacksmiths and carpenters, jewelers and leather workers. As a result there were several industries that thrived during their time. The Danes (Vikings inhabitants of Dublin) were slowly converted into Christianity with the first Bishop being appointed in 1028. The Vikings ruled Dublin for almost three centuries until they were defeated by the Irish in 1014.

Then Dublin became the center of English power in Ireland in 1169-71. During the Medieval years from 1171 onwards, Dublin was a tightly knit place with around 5,000 to 10,000 people. Strongbow, the Earl of Pembroke, a Norman (Vikings who settled in Northern France) helped the English rulers to capture Dublin in 1171. Between 1172 and 1191, the Cathedral of Christchurch was rebuilt. In 1190, Dublin was devastated by fire but was soon rebuilt. The Normans built a wooden fortress in Dublin and in the early 13th century, it was rebuilt in stone strengthening the walls surrounding the castle.

Trade and commerce thrived in 1200's, with goods being imported and exported from various European countries. There were weekly markets in Dublin, where people from all over the country would come to buy and sell wares and other necessities. A conduit was built to bring in fresh water to Dublin in 1224 and in the 14th century, the main streets were paved. Sanitation was one lingering issue in Dublin as there were no sewerage system at the time.

Dublin went through several upheavals in the 16th and 17th centuries, but The Reformation (a schism within Western Christianity), occured peacefully in Dublin during this era. It was also during this period that Dublin prospered with their living standards rising to impressive levels. Like all 16th century towns, Dublin suffered from outbreaks of plague. In 1579, an outbreak killed thousands and another tragedy befell Dublinin 1596 when a gunpowder store exploded killing more than 120 people.

In 1591, Trinity College was founded by Queen Elizabeth granting the charter for this prestigious educational institution. In the year 1700, the population grew to about 60,000 and the conditions in the middle and upper classes improved although there were still traces of poverty around.

Multiple structures such as the Marsh Library and St Ann's Church were built and a number of hospitals were founded. Several parks like College Park in 1722, Phoenix Park in the mid-18th century, Reanelagh gardens in 1776, Botanic Gardens in 1795 and the St Stephens Green in the late 18th century, all provided fashionable places to relax and take leisurely walks within Dublin.

By the 1800's, the population grew to about 180,000 and along with it fever hospitals were opened in Dublin. The most common fever during this time was typhus, sometimes called goal fever and it afflicted many of the poor due to their living conditions. The Great Famine in 1845 also affected Dublin in a harrowing way. The numbers of those fleeing due to starvation was overwhelming and the death toll shot up to hundreds of thousands throughout Ireland.

In the early 19th century, several new bridges were built across the Liffey. Amenities greatly improved in Dublin during the 19th century and in the 20th century, several rebellions and uprisings took place. In the early 1900 Dublin suffered severely from street fighting and many buildings were destroyed. The War of Independence took place, a conflict which produced many tragic incidents, a number of which are still remembered today. The Anglo-Irish Treaty between Britain and Ireland was signed, creating the Irish Free State.

Ireland as a country remained neutral during the Second World War. The war years also saw the temporary increase of the Jewish community who fled from the German Nazis.

It was in the 1960's that progress was made to remove tenements where Dublin's working class populace dwelled, replacing them with suburban housing estates around the edge of the city. In the late 20th century, traditional industries such as textiles, brewing and distilling declined, but the city council built new industrial estates on the outskirts of the city and new industries like electronics, chemicals and engineering sprung forth.

Dublin celebrated its millennium in 1988 and with its booming economy it attracted immigrants from all over the world. Today, Dublin's population is approximately 505,000 and growing.

For a place that went through many struggles and challenges, each time rising up to victory, Dublin earned a remarkable heirloom of mixed traditions and cultures. This resulted in a very unique composition of the present-day Dubliner's way of life. As young as the majority of the current population are, their free-spirited nature soars high and there is no way to go but forward, with a clear vision of a carefully mapped out direction for their future.

Climate

Dublin's climate is very similar to that of northwest Europe. It has a maritime temperate climate with less rainfall than the rest of the "Emerald Isles". Dublin has mild winters and cool summers and lacks temperature extremes.

Spring

From February to April, Dublin blooms with spring as the city experiences the driest months with the weather still being quite cold. The average highest temperatures range from 46 to 54°F (8 to 12 °C), with April considered particularly pleasant.

Summer

Summer months are from May until early September. During these months, the weather is cool and pleasant with temperatures peaking at around 68°F (20°C) in July but the sun shines best in May and June. Rainfall is very common in this season, but the warmest months, July and August, get about 18 hours of daylight and it gets dark only after 11pm.

Autumn

From August to October, highest temperature reaches between 64 and 57°F (18 and 14°C). September is considered a mild, temperate month. These are the mid-season months for travellers where you can enjoy Dublin with the bronze-burnished leaves around.

Winter

Winter is very damp and showers are common all throughout the season. A few flurries may occur, but snow is unlikely. January and February are the coldest months when the temperature gets not more than 3.5°C (37-41°F). December is the wettest month and the city gets around 80mm of precipitation.

Best Time to Visit

The best time to visit Dublin is in the warm summer months between May and August. February is the month which receives the least rainfall on average, but it is almost impossible to avoid some rain in Dublin. The off-peak months are significantly cheaper, so if you are travelling on a budget, it's best to consider visiting Dublin in spring, autumn or even winter.

Language

English is the language widely spoken in Dublin. Street signs and official buildings are signposted in both English and Gaelic, the indigenous Irish language, although you rarely hear them speak Gaelic. Dubliners are very friendly and mildly inquisitive. They can strike a casual conversation with just about anyone, on the streets, in pubs or anywhere. They are also known for their sharp wit and deadpan humour.

Getting In

Major airlines from all over the world fly to Dublin airport regularly. There are now direct flights from seven major US airports. Dublin is one of the few airports offering "border preclearance" services for US-bound passengers.

Passengers coming in from long distance destinations like Asia, Africa and Central America, may need to take connecting flights to Dublin via

London airports or another major European terminal such as Frankfurt, Munich, Paris or Amsterdam. There are around 50 scheduled flights daily to and from Dublin from other airports.

For more information on flight schedules, you may visit: http://www.dublin.info/flights/

Getting Around

Dublin is a city divided into two, cut into half by the Liffey River. The Northside and the Southside. Getting around is easy enough considering its size. To locate an address, postal codes will help you find what you are looking for. Odd numbers are on the Northside and even numbers are on the Southside, and one hint for travelers is, the higher the number, the further away the location will be from the city center. Also, keep in mind that several of the city's national museums and galleries are free. Always check out their websites for more information or call in advance for reservations.

Restaurants in the city also promote "early-bird" specials. Keep an eye on their boards and posters displayed on their windows. For your shopping needs, key places are Henry Street on the Northside and Grafton Street on the Southside. For bargain-hunters, there are shops on the side streets like "Flip" and "Wildchild", both in the Temple Bar.

There are several forms of transportation which can take you to any point in the city. Buses or trams traverse the different routes within the city.

Licensed taxi cabs can be hailed at any point, taking you to the destination of your choice.

DART(Dublin Area Rapid Transit) is a light-rail network that goes through the city center and serves many of Dublin's coastal suburbs. LUAS is the newest mode of transportation in the city. It is also a light rail tram system with two operating lines, Red and Green. The most useful stops are on the Red Line as it serves both Dublin's main train stations and has a stop at the Museum of Decorative Arts and History.

There are also a number of bus tours offering a "hop-on, hop off" tours like Dublin Bus Tours, but the best way to explore Dublinis by bicycle. For the most part, Dublin is fairly flat with a few, modest climbs and you can park your bike anywhere, though you will find dedicated parking spots in many city center locations. Bike hires are also available.

Public Bicycle Schemes. Photo by Public Bicycle Schemes

For more information, you may visit:
http://www.dublin.info/getting-around/

2 DUBLIN'S HISTORIC NORTHSIDE

Dublin City, O'Connell Street. Photo by William Murphy

The first day of a Dublin tour will start at the Northside where you can feast on a multitude of sights, exploring the rich culture and sites of Dublin. It would be wise to ensure a full tummy before heading off to see some of the sites.

Northside has a small, unpretentious cafe called Brother Hubbard. It is a small, owner-run coffee shop serving great coffee and good food. They also have a wide selection of baked goodies that you can choose from. You will find that this is a great place to plan a busy day ahead.

Brother Hubbard

153 Capel Street, Dublin 1, Ireland

+353 1 441 1112

The Northside is where you can find the city's main thoroughfare called O'Connell Street, spanning from Parnell Square, all the way to the Liffey. Halfway down O'Connell, is the GPO or the General Post Office. Along Henry Street off O'Connell is a popular shopping district where you stop by for delicious goods.

For those who wish to buy from fresh harvests, a traditional vegetable market is just around the corner along Moore Street. Many museums, theatres, parks and restaurants are also located here. Northside offers visitors a chance to catch a glimpse of a Dubliner's daily life, complete with the hustle and bustle of their usual fare and activities. Let's get started with an itinerary for your first day in Dublin.

Dublin Writers Museum

Get to know how the Irish became known for their written gift of gab. Visit Dublin Writers Museum to learn why literature is their highest form of art. Located right at the heart of Dublin City Center is a gallery that showcases the most illustrious masterpieces of Ireland. This museum was opened in 1991 and is devoted to preserving the rich literary tradition up to 1970. Read through the priceless collection that includes works of Dublin's literary celebrities like Swift and Sheridan, Shaw and Wilde, Yeats, Joyce and Beckett, to name a few.

The Writers Museum. Dublin, Ireland. Photo by Charles16e

Their works are presented through their books, letters, portraits and personal items. The building is comprised of two 18th century houses, an upstairs gallery, library and a Zen garden. There is also a museum cafe and a basement restaurant aptly called, Chapter One, which serves contemporary Irish cuisine.

As the capital of Ireland, Dublin remains known as

the city of writers and literature and this museum can definitely let you discover, explore and simply enjoy the city's literary heritage.

Additional Information:

18 North Parnell Square, Dublin City Center

+353 187 22077

Operating hours: 10am-5pm Mon-Sat, 11am -5pm Sun

Price: adult/child €7.50/4.70

The National Leprechaun Museum

Let out the childish spirit within you in this place which offers an interesting interactive presentation of Irish folklore and stories dedicated to the world of Irish myth and traditions. Be prepared to take on the journey in the world of imagination as the story teller walks you through the world of leprechaun and fairies via themed rooms. This is a break from the usual museum guided tours and will give you quite a different experience.

Additional Information:

Twilfit House Jervis Street, Dublin 1, Ireland

+353 1 873 3899

Operating hours: 10am to 5:45pm Mon to Sun

St Michan's Church

St. Michan's Catholic Church. Photo by <u>*William Murphy*</u>

A sacred destination built on the site of a Danish chapel founded in 1095, this church served as the only parish church on this side of the Liffey. It was built to serve the Viking population expelled from within the city walls. This church was rebuilt in 1685 and is now one of the popular attractions in Dublin.

Getting inside the church will let you see its notable interiors of fine woodwork, a large organ from 1724, a Penitent's Stool, and a chalice dating from 1516. But the main highlight that should not be missed here is the burial vault located underneath the church. If you have the interest and the nerve to do it, try exploring this part of the church. Here, centuries-old bodies remain intact because of the dry atmosphere. Dusty corpses are lined up in open coffins and legend has it that Bram Stoker's Dracula was inspired in part by his frequent childhood visits to this vault.

Additional Information:

Church Street

Dublin 7, Ireland

+353 1 872 4154

Dublinia

Dublina. Photo by Laura Bittner

Discover Dublin's colorful history by a visit to this heritage center located at the heart of a medieval city Dublin featuring 3 exhibitions. The first is "Viking Dublin" which will take the visitors back to life in the city during the Viking times. Get on board a Viking warship, take a trip down a Viking street, see burial customs and explore the Viking legacy and more. The second exhibition is the "Medieval Dublin" which will let you see the typical Medieval way of life which includes a busy medieval market, a rich merchant's house and a noisy medieval street. Lastly, there is the "History Hunters" exhibition which features how we came to know of Dublin's past. See magnificent artifacts on display including those found at the famous Wood Quay excavation.

Dublinia also features a historical reenactment, with actors playing the roles of Vikings and Medieval Dubliners (in full costume).

This exhibition opened in 1993 and was redeveloped in 2010 and currently attracts a large number of visitors per month.

Additional Information:

St Michaels Hill

Christchurch

+353 1 679 4611

Operating hours: 10am to 5:30pm Mon-Sun

GAA Museum – Croke Park

Dubliners have always been known for their love of sports. The GAA (Gaelic Athletic Association) Museum founded the 19th century, was created to foster the development of "hurling" or the Irish Field . It showcases their love for this game by exhibition galleries illustrating the story of Gaelic games from ancient times to the present day. There is a vast collection of sporting artifacts which include hurleys, jerseys, trophies, medals, programmes, publications and banners.You may even test your hurling and football skills in the interactive games zone.

Croke Park on the other hand, is the iconic stadium which serves as the heart of Irish sporting life for over 100 years. This sports arena has been the venue of many Irish national hurling and Gaelic football games.

Additional Information:

Cusack Stand

St. Joseph's Avenue

Croke Park, Dublin 3

Ireland

+353 1 819 2323

Museum is open 9:30am – 5:00pm Mon-Sat, 10:30am – 5:00pm Sun

Old Jameson Distillery

The Old Jameson Distillery. Photo by Neil Turner

Add more information to your knowledge bank by visiting an Irish whiskey distillery now serving as a tourist attraction. This is the original site, where the famous Jameson Irish Whiskey was distilled until 1971. Set in the heart of Dublin, a visit to this distillery will be a very engaging experience as visitors are taken on guided tours explaining the history of Jameson Irish Whiskey, the different stages of whiskey making, and a video of what the distillery was like when the founder, John Jameson, was still alive. Part of the tour will be a tutored whiskey tasting and feel free to unwind at the bar, restaurant or pick up something for your envious friends at the gift shop.

The distillery is laid out over two floors and sits above the original fermentation vats which can now be seen through the glass door in the atrium.

Additional Information:

Bow Street

Smithfield Village

Dublin 7, Ireland

+353 1 807 2355

3 DUBLIN'S VIBRANT SOUTHSIDE

Your second day in this great city can be spent exploring the other side of Dublin, the Southside. There is no better way to start the day than by having breakfast at Bewley's Grafton Street Cafe. Savor the best coffee in Ireland, hand roasted in this coffee shop. They also serve cakes and other delectable items like salads, pizzas, pastas and more, all freshly made and served in magnificent surroundings.

Bewley's Grafton Street Cafe

78- 79 Grafton St

Dublin, Ireland

+353 1 672 7720

Now it's time to get back on track. The other side of Dublin, the Southside which is known to be the affluent side, houses galleries and a posh shopping area along Grafton Street. This is where you can find trendy, signature shops. The famous bohemian Temple Bar can also be found here. Not to be missed will be Saint Stephens Green, a delightful park with an intriguing history that now provides respite to urban dwellers and visitors alike. The Southside is also home to Ireland's oldest and most famous university, Trinity College, the Government buildings, Dublin Castle, Lansdowne Road Stadium and Christchurch Cathedral and St Patrick's Cathedral. Without further ado, let's dive into day two!

Christ Church Cathedral

Christ Church Cathedral. Photo by William Murphy

One of the key places to see in Dublin is the Christ Church Cathedral. This church, also known as The Cathedral of the Holy Trinity, sits in the oldest part of the city, dating back to 1038 AD. The wooden structure was first built by Sitric, the then Danish king of Dublin and in 1171 it was extended into a cruciform and rebuilt into stone by Strongbow. In 1878 huge restoration was done where only the transepts, the crypt and a few other portions were preserved.

The interiors of this church has magnificent stoneworks and graceful pointed arches, with delicately chiselled columns. This beautiful edifice has stained glass windows and smaller chapels behind the main altar. This is always a must-see for visitors to Dublin.

Additional Information:

Christchurch Place

Dublin 8, Ireland

+353 1 677 8099

Guinness Storehouse

Enjoy the world's most famous brew right at its birthplace ! A Dublin trip will never be complete without dropping by the home of the world famous beer, the black stuff or stout as they call it. A massive seven-storey building, the brewery and fermentation plant has been remodelled into the shape of a giant pint of Guinness. Visitors are provided with the information of how the drink is made, its history and a lot more.

Cheers! Dublin Style. Photo by <u>*Zach Dischner*</u>

The tour is highlighted by the final stop at the Gravity Bar located at the top most floor of the building where guests are offered a complimentary pint of Guinness, and they can savor the drink while relaxing and enjoying the breathtaking 360-degree view of Dublin City.

Additional Information:

St. James's Gate

Dublin 8, Ireland

+353 1 408 4800

Trinity College

Travel down memory lane as you explore Ireland's

most prestigious university. Trinity College has always been recognized for academic excellence and transformative student experiences for many years.

Trinity College. Photo by Fred

During the early years, the majority of the students who attended this institution were predominantly rich, Protestant males but times have changed since then, and in recent years, the majority of the student populace are now female Catholics.

It is a masterpiece of architecture with beautifully laid out landscaping in Georgian aspic. Walk though the cobbled stone pathways which will bring you back to 18th century setting.

Inside the Old Library building, guests can marvel at the "Turning Darkness into Light" exhibition, then head to the Treasury where the Book of Kells can be found. This lavishly decorated treasure is an illuminated 9th century manuscript Gospel book in Latin, containing the four Gospels of the New Testament. After this, you may then proceed upstairs to the Long Room which houses 200,000 of the Library's oldest books in its oak staircases.

This library is known to have one of the best and largest collections in the world. You can also find here a rare original edition of the proclamation of the Independent Irish Republic of the 19th century.

Another distinguished national icon stored here is Ireland's oldest surviving harp from the 15th century which is currently featured in the Euro coin as Ireland's national symbol. Marble busts of the great philosophers and writers of the western world line the Long Room.

Officially named as University of Dublin, Elizabeth I granted its charter in 1592.

Additional Information:

Dublin, Ireland

+353 1 896 1000

Opening hours: 8am -10pm

The National Gallery of Ireland

Right across the road from Trinity College is this gallery which is well worth a visit. Be awed with the gallery's national collection of Irish and European arts. Today the collection includes over 2,500 paintings and some 10,000 other works in different media including watercolours, drawings, prints and sculpture.

Photo by Kate

Every major European School of painting is extensively represented. It also houses a renowned collection of Irish paintings. The gallery's highlights include works by Vermeer, Caravaggio, Picasso, Van Gogh and Monet.

Additional Information:

Merrion Square & Clare Street

Dublin 2, Ireland

+353 1 632 5133

Opening hours: 9:30am to 5:30pm, Mon-Sun

Phoenix Park

Located right at the heart of the city is the Phoenix Park. One of Europe's largest city parks, which covers 1,752 acres or 707 hectares of land space, this is one of the city's best-loved free amenities. It is a 350-year old place of leisure which started as a royal deer park for King Charles II in 1662. Archaeologists have discovered that a Neolithic community lived on a high strip at the Southern edge of this park circa 5,500 years ago.

This is where you can find Dublin Zoo, the home of many rare and exotic animals living and roaming in a wide variety of natural habitats. Around one-third of the park is covered with deciduous trees like oak, ash, lime, beech, sycamore and horse chestnut. It has 50 per cent of the mammal species and 40 per cent of the bird species in Ireland, making it one of the most biodiverse locations in the country.

See many rare and exotic animals living and roaming in a wide variety of natural habitats. Wander through the African Savannah and gaze at the giraffes, zebras, scimitar oryx and ostrich, then head to the Kaziranga Forest to see the magnificent herd of Asian elephants that call this beautiful place home. Dublin Zoo, located in the Phoenix Park in the heart of Dublin City, allows you to discover amazing animals that include tigers, hippos, bats, rare monkeys, gorillas, chimpanzees, red pandas and reptiles, to name but a few!

Additional Information:

Dublin 8, Ireland

+353 1 474 8900

Kilmainham Gaol

Kilmainham Gaol. Photo by psyberartist

Set foot in a place rich in history with a visit to Dublin's famous historical site. A political prison, this place stood as a silent witness to countless persecutions and execution of many Irish heroes of the past which include the seven signatories of the proclamation of the Irish Independent Republic. This is also one of the largest unoccupied gaols or jails in Europe, covering some of the most heroic and tragic events in Ireland's emergence as a modern nation from 1780s to the 1920s.

Attractions include a major exhibition detailing the political and penal history of the prison and its restoration. The tour of the prison includes an audio-visual show. Tours may be arranged for visitors with special needs by prior arrangement. It is advisable to book in advance as there is a large number of daily visitors.

Additional Information:

Inchicore Road, Kilmainham

Dublin 8

+353 453 5984

This is open everyday between 9:30am to 6:00pm.

4 DUBLIN'S CULTURAL TREATS

Take sometime to sit down and relish in the last two day's adventure, experience and knowledge, as you savor the goodness of a traditional Irish breakfast. Odessa is an awesome place to have brunch before spending the last day in Dublin. Grab some bite of their mouthful brunch classics, Full Irish, Eggs Benedict, Steak Sandwich and a lot more. These treats will go perfectly with coffee or juices. After a hearty meal, it will be time to soak with cultural treats as well.

Odessa

14 Dame Court, City Centre South

Dublin 2, Ireland

+353 (0)1 670-7634

Dublin's Castle

This castle was built in the 13th century on a site previously settled by the Vikings. In the middle ages, the original castle served as a fortress. At some point it functioned as a prison, treasury, courts of law and the seat of the English Administration for 700 years.

Dublin Castle. Photo by William Murphy

The British formally handed power over to the Irish in a stirring ceremony right in the castle's courtyard. Dublin Castle is now used for state functions, receptions and inaugurations. On occasion, Dublin Castle may be closed to the public to give way to government business so it would be advisable to call first before visiting.

Additional Information:

Dame Street

Dublin 2, Ireland

+353 1 645 8813

Opening hours: 9:45am – 4:45pm, Mon to Sat;
12pm to 4:45pm, Sun

Chester Beatty Library

Inside Dublin Castle is another gem of discovery. Described by travel guides as "not just the best museum in Ireland, but one of the best in Europe", it is an art museum and library which houses the great collection of manuscripts, miniature paintings, prints, drawings, rare books and decorative arts assembled by Sir Alfred Chester Beatty (1875-1968).

Its rich collections from countries across Asia, the Middle East, North Africa and Europe opens a window to the artistic treasures of the great cultures and religions of the world. Egyptian papyrus texts, beautifully illuminated copies of the Qur'an, the Bible, European Medieval and Renaissance manuscripts are among the highlights of the collection.

In its diversity, the collection captures much of the richness of human creative expression from about 2700 B.C to the present day. Facilities include, restaurant, gift and book shop, audio visual presentations, roof garden and baby-changing facilities.

Additional Information:

Dublin Castle

Dublin 2, Ireland

+353 1 407 0750

Opening Hours: 10am – 5pm, Mon to Fri; 11am – 5:00pm, Sat; 1pm – 5pm, Sun

St. Stephen's Green

St. Stephen's Green. Photo by William Murphy

Step into Ireland's best known Victorian park with an extensive perimeter fence and shrub planting, as well as spectacular summer and spring Victorian bedding. The herbaceous border also provides colour from early spring to late autumn. The park has over 3.5 km of accessible pathways. The waterfalls and Pulham rock work on the western side should not be missed as well as the ornamental lake which provides home for waterfowl and a garden for the visually impaired.

This park was enclosed in 1664 and around the park Georgian buildings of neo classical architecture and design were constructed. These served as residences for the affluent society of the bygone glorious years. These are marks of a grandiose era where structures are stately, uniformed and follow symmetrical patterns. Doors of this residences are painted in lively colors which complements the blooms and foliage of St. Stephen's Green. Today, people troop to the green to sit down and enjoy the relaxing scenery.

Additional Information:

Dublin 2, Ireland

+353 1 475 7816

National Aquatic Center

One of the country's pride is this principal facility for water sports built in 2003 as it hosted that year's Special Olympics World Summer Games. Inside the center is AquaZone, one of the most innovative water parks in Europe.

Alone, or with family and friends, there's a whole host of exciting features to ensure fun-filled thrills and activities for everyone. If you crave extreme thrills, raging water adventures, flying through the air, or just an enjoyable family day out in Dublin, AquaZone at the National Aquatic Centre has Europe's biggest and best water rides and attractions waiting for you!

Additional Information:

Snugborough Road

Blanchardstown

Dublin 15, Ireland

+353 1 646 4300

Farmleigh House

Farmleigh. Photo by William Murphy

This is an official Irish State guest house which was formerly one of the Dublin residences of the

Guinness family. Situated in an elevated position above the River Liffey, the estate spans 78 acres of expensive private gardens with stands of mature cypress, pine and oak trees, a boating pond, walled garden, sunken garden, out offices and a herd of the rare Kerry cattle.

Built in the late 18th century, Farmleigh was purchased by Edward Cecil Guinness, a great-grandson of Arthur Guinness, in 1873. The house contains many beautiful features including the Main House area (a fine example of Georgian-Victorian architecture), the Sunken Garden, the Walled Garden, the famous Clock Tower and the Lake and The Benjamin Iveagh Library. The library holds some of the finest examples of Irish bookbinding from the 18th, 19th and 20th centuries. The collection was donated to Marsh's Library by the Guinness family.

Additional Information:

Phoenix Park

Dublin 15, Ireland

+353 1 815 5900

St Patrick's Cathedral

Built between 1220 and 1260, in honor of Ireland's patron saint, Saint Patrick's Cathedral is one of the few buildings left from the medieval city of Dublin.

Today, St Patrick's is the National Cathedral for the Church of Ireland and still the largest cathedral in Ireland.

St. Patrick's Cathedral. Photo by Miguel Mendez

Visitors can learn about the building's fascinating history, including its most famous Dean (head) Jonathan Swift, who is one of around 700 burials on site.

Additional Information:

Saint Patrick's Close

Dublin 8, Ireland

+353 1 453 9472

5 BEST PLACES (EAT, WINE & DINE)

Ham hock. Photo by Jessica Spengler

Dublin is a place teeming with different venues for gastronomic feasts and culinary delights. The choice can be endless depending on one's preference but here are some of the top suggestions.

Restaurant Patrick Guilbaud

This is one of the most respected restaurants in the

whole of Ireland. It opened in 1981 and boasts of an impressive wine list and food choices featuring contemporary french cuisine. Menu highlights include Clogher Head lobster ravioli, caramelized veal sweetbreads and the assiette au chocolat. Their main dining room has charming interiors and they have a heated terrace looking over the 16th century garden of The Merrion Hotel with a charming spot for dining.

Additional Information:

21 Upper Merrion Street

Dublin 2, Ireland

+353 1 676 4192

Thornton's

Located inside Fitzwilliam Hotel, this French restaurant enjoys a splendid view of St. Stephen's Green and serves delectable cuisines which include the Bere Island scallops with truffi e mousse and the sea urchin with brunoise of vegetables. They also have an eight-course menu surprise devised for your table. Here you will find a stylish dining room as well as a chic Canape Lounge. Private dining can be arranged.

Additional Information:

128 St. Stephen's Green

Dublin 2, Ireland

+353 1 478 7008

The Winding Stair

This is one of the places where one can enjoy traditional Irish fares. This buzzy little eatery has long been a favorite of the locals and tourists. All ingredients are locally sourced and organically grown. They also serve delicious seafood and they boast of a superb selection of Irish farmhouse cheeses and cured meats. The setting is quite unique with bookcase-lined walls providing good company while enjoying good food and excellent wine. You may try their Dingle Bay crab on soda bread or an Ummera bacon-wrapped pork fillet with roasted onion mash, savoy cabbage and apple gravy. One thing that you should not miss is their famous bread and butter pudding with whiskey sauce.

Additional Information:

40 Ormond Quay

Dublin 1, Ireland

+353 1 872 7320

Gallagher's Boxty House

A real tourist haunt but is still worth checking out. It serves traditional Irish food served with a modern twist. The word Boxty in its name actually derived from a form of Irish soup which you may want to try. Check out their fantastic menu which goes well with beer.

Additional Information:

20-21 Temple Bar

Dublin 2, Ireland

+353 1 677 2762

Green 19

Not far from the main party areas of Dublin, this restaurant offers exquisite food at very affordable prices. They have a wide array of modern dishes served in a setting with cool decor. You cannot book ahead in advance so just make sure to come in early to beat the queues.

Additional Information:

19 Camden Street Lower

Dublin 2, Ireland

+353 1 478 9626

6 A TASTE OF DUBLIN'S NIGHTLIFE

The Temple Bar. Photo by <u>Tobias Abel</u> CC BY-ND 2.0

For a different kind of nightlife, Dublin has their fair share of theatres & live productions, so enjoy going out to watch them. Dublin has many festivals, with St. Patrick's Day as the most celebrated. This is a good time to have fun while partying in Dublin (which can be a bit costly) gets to a peak. It's not the only festival Dublin has to offer though. Keep an eye out for Dun Laoghaire Festival of International Cultures in August and the Dun Laoghaire Regatta in May.

Likewise, Marley Park offers a series of free open-air events throughout the year and there's an event known as the "Taste of Dublin," held in Iveagh Park which happens every summer. There, visitors can sample all the best food that Dublin has to offer while being entertained by a varied group of Irish and international musicians.

And of course, Dublin is known for downing some pints and to date, it has over 600 pubs across the city. The main ones can be found in Temple Bar, at the heart of the city and is also the known as Dublin's nightlife center. Here, you can see all those beer drinking hotspots where you can do the "pub crawl" – which means, to hop from one pub to another (at least 3), where you will enjoy the pint while listening to Irish traditional music. Just be ready as most pubs in Temple Bar are always full of tourists. If you want to mix with some locals though, here are some of the suggested spots.

The Brazen Head

This is Ireland's oldest pub dating back to 1198. Just a short walk from Christchurch Cathedral and Guinness Brewery. This is also a place to hear and experience the best of Irish music and storytelling while enjoying both traditional and contemporary dishes.

Additional Information:

20 Bridge Street Lower

Dublin 8, Ireland

+353 1 677 9549

The Dawson Lounge

Dubbed as the smallest lounge in the city, this place is quite a gem. It has 70's decor in wood panel finish with a very nice atmosphere of a traditional Irish pub. You will get a sense of adventure the moment you walk in the door. The Dawson Louonge has a very unassuming presence and they serve the cheapest pint in town.

Additional Information:

25 Dawson Street

Dublin 2, Ireland

+353 1 671 0311

Central Hotel Library Bar

This is a place where everything around you is enchanting. This bar combines the charm and elegance with modern facilities. Enjoy your favorite drinks in a place designed to give you a haven of peaceful luxury. The bar itself is simple but the room is beautifully refined with couches, armchairs, coffee tables and cabinets full of hardbacks, their covers fashioned with stitching. This bar is one of the most relaxed places and an ideal venues to unwind.

Additional Information:

Exchequer Street

Dublin, Ireland

+353 1 679 7302

The Market Bar

Walk through an open-air heated courtyard with tables and chairs, leading into a vast luminous warehouse. Inside the sky-lit interiors are red-brick walls, tall plants and rustic wooden benches. This place has a warm, earthy effect and is a favorite hang out of the locals. This was Dublin's original gastro bar and foremost tapas restaurant. They have an extensive cuisine and must-try will be of course, tapas grazed in olives and dips and their chicken chorizo skewers.

Additional Information:

14A Fade Street

Dublin 2, Ireland

+353 1 613 9094

O'Donoghue's

Share in the beat of authentic Irish music and let this experience stay with you long after you've left the place. Here, the music is played live before you, while you sip and enjoy your favorite pint. This place has a rich heritage and stands on a very historical site in Dublin. This is also a favorite haunt for Dubliners.

Additional Information:

15 Merrion Row

Dublin 2, Ireland

+353 1 660 7194

7 BEST PLACES TO STAY (LUXURIOUS, MID-RANGE, BUDGET)

Dublin, Shelbourne Hotel. Photo by [David McSpadden](#)

Luxurious

The Merrion Hotel Dublin

Located in the heart of Dublin city center, this is the capital's most luxurious five star hotel. It has 142 stylish and elegantly designed bedrooms and suites. With Giorgian-inspired interiors and decors, The Merrion offers exquisite comfort with relaxed elegance in its world-class facilities and amenities.

Additional Information:

Upper Merrion St

Dublin2, Ireland

+353 1 603 0600

Shelbourne Hotel

A Rennaisance hotel also considered to be a national treasure, this was built in 1824. This five-star hotel is right at the heart of the city center, overlooking St. Stephen's Green. This hotel offers spacious accommodations, 265 well-appointed rooms with the luxurious Egyptian cotton bedding, on top of other elegant amenities and facilities.

Additional Information:

27 St. Stephen's Green

Dublin, Ireland

+353 1 663 4500

The Westbury

A Dublin icon, located between Trinity College and St. Stephen's Green its right at the heart of the cultural quarter, with its endless restaurants and shopping options. It has a fine dining restaurant,

Wilde, which serves international cuisines using only the best local ingredients. This luxurious hotel has world-class facilities and amenities with 187 well-appointed rooms and 18 elegant suites. It takes pride for being known for its culinary excellence and also the home of one of Ireland's most stunning privately-owned art collections, including pieces by Sir John Lavery and Louis le Brocquy.

Additional Information:

Grafton Street

Dublin 2, Ireland

+353 1 679 1122

Mid-range

The Beacon

This 4-star luxury hotel is conveniently situated near Dundrum and Leopardstown. It is just a few minutes from Ireland's most prestigious shopping experience of Dundrum Town Center. This fabulous hotel has a modern chic decor, modern, funky style and ambience. It has spacious, stylish rooms, a fitness studio, a Thai Restaurant and a bar. Ambience is generally welcoming and relaxing giving you a stunning boutique hotel experience.

Additional Information:

Beacon Court

Dublin 18, Ireland

+353 1 643 7064

Waterloo House

One of Dublin's most charming place, this hotel is situated in Ballsbridge Dublin 4, near the bustling Baggot Street and only a few minutes walk from St. Stephen's Green, Grafton Street and many of Dublin's key places of interest. Two tall Giorgian townhouses to offer the finest in luxury four star boutique accommodation, in an elegant, stylish ambience, in a quiet residential street with gardens on both sides. IT has 19 well-appointed rooms with 24-hour service and reception.

Additional Information:

10 Waterloo Road

Dublin 4, Ireland

+353 1 660 1888

Schoolhouse Hotel

Dubbed as the "hidden gem" of Dublin, this four-star hotel is a favorite hotel for locals and international visitors alike. Originally a school house in 1859, this hotel have witnessed many of Dublin's historical events including the 1016 Uprising. The walls of this hotel have many stories to tell. Each of the 31 individual boutique rooms are named after some of Ireland's most important and influential people.

For nearly two centuries, this hotel has stood as a landmark on the banks of Dublin's Grand Canal.

Additional Information:

2-8 Northumberland Road

Ballsbridge, Dublin 4, Ireland

+353 1 667 5014

Budget

Abigail's Hotel

One of the top hostels in Dublin, this is located in Ashton Quay, overlooking the Liffey River. It is also near the major attractions in the city as well as the shopping districts. All rooms are complete and accommodation comes with free breakfast. They have a friendly and knowledgeable staff who will be eager to provide you with a warm service.

Additional Information:

7-9 Aston Quay

Dublin 2, Ireland

+353 1 677 9007

Beresford Hotel

Formerly known to locals as Hotel Isaacs, it had recently undergone renovations and was renamed as Beresford Hotel. It has 103 rooms, all budget-friendly and these rooms come in two varieties: the modern business-class type, with crisp duvets, ruby red throws and round table of blond wood, and the Georgian rooms which are more fancy, with overstuffed chairs, ottomans, and dainty bedside lamps. This is a wise pick for travellers because of its good location, warm service and reasonable rates.

Additional Information:

Gardiner Street Lower

Dublin, Ireland

+353 1 813 4700

Barnacles Hostel

Located at the heart of Temple Bar, it offers an excellent location especially if you really want to get the best of drinking yourself green. It offers 149 beds, all simple and compact, in splashes of color and unmatched patterns. All rooms have private bedrooms.

Additional Information:

19 Temple Lane South

Dublin, Ireland

+353 1 671 6277

8 OTHER RECOMMENDED PLACES TO VISIT

Sorrento Terrace from Hawk Cliff, Killiney, Co. Dublin, Ireland. Photo by Giuseppe Milo

Venture South along Dublin Bay and come to some of Dublin's most picturesque spots. The scenery changes rapidly from flat sandy beaches to rocky cliffs and coves harbouring picture perfect seaside towns and harbours. Sandycove, Dalkey and Killiney have preserved an old world charm. On a sunny day, you can even find an almost Mediterranean atmosphere here. To the North of

Dublin you find Howth, a major fishing harbour and Malahide, a quaint seaside town with a park and romantic 19th century castle.

Newgrange. Photo by Sharon Drummond

There are also day trips out of Dublin that visitors can enjoy. Newgrange is a 5,000 year old burial tomb which can offer a truly unique experience. Glendalough is a monastic site located in a stunning valley near a lake. Both of these sites are UNESCO protected structures and can be reached by bus from the city center.

CONCLUSION

The capital of the Emerald Isles (a poetic name given to Ireland due to its green countryside), Dublin epitomizes fun and free spirit with a well earned reputation as being a party city since the nightlife is one of its greatest attractions. However, the city has more to offer than just booze and jollity. It boasts of rich heritage with its many cultural and historical attractions.

It will be interesting to get to know the facts surrounding its existence, how the early inhabitants lived and how the city evolved into what it is today. The many highlights in its history provided many peaks and valleys lending colors and spice to an otherwise drab and dragging years. They have a engaging culture and history, a very unique past which is still very much alive in every Dubliner's heart. They are a proud race on the midst of an energetic economic boom, trying to retain as much of their heritage as possible.

They have a long-standing love affair with literature and you can see this evidently showcased in almost every part of the city. Their music is one of a kind and emits a kind of happy feeling as if matching the gaiety and pride of the Dubliner's hearts. As Oscar Wilde says, "Ordinary riches can be stolen; real riches cannot. In your soul are infinitely precious things that cannot be taken from you." It may somehow tell you about Dubliners, for their beloved city is rich in precious things that no one can ever take away.

MORE FROM THIS AUTHOR

Below you'll find some of our other books that are popular on Amazon and Kindle as well. Alternatively, you can visit our author page on Amazon to see other work done by us.

3 Day Guide to Berlin: A 72-hour definitive guide on what to see, eat and enjoy in Berlin, Germany

3 Day Guide to Vienna: A 72-hour definitive guide on what to see, eat and enjoy in Vienna Austria

3 Day Guide to Santorini: A 72-hour definitive guide on what to see, eat and enjoy in Santorini Greece

3 Day Guide to Provence: A 72-hour definitive guide on what to see, eat and enjoy in Provence, France

3 Day Guide to Istanbul: A 72-hour definitive guide on what to see, eat and enjoy in Istanbul, Turkey

3 Day Guide to Budapest: A 72-hour Definitive Guide on What to See, Eat and Enjoy in Budapest, Hungary

3 Day Guide to Venice: A 72-hour Definitive Guide on What to See, Eat and Enjoy in Venice, Italy

3 Day Guide to Singapore: A 72-hour Definitive Guide on What to See, Eat and Enjoy in Singapore, Singapore

17468229R00042

Printed in Great Britain
by Amazon